BALD EAGLE HANDBOOK

A Guide To Watching Wintering American Bald Eagles

With Self-Guide

Eagle Watching Maps of

St. Charles County, MO
Madison County, IL
Calhoun County, IL
Jersey County, IL

by Larry Wright

Grafton, Illinois

Published by
Gallinipper Enterprises
#1 Tara Point Estates
Box 640
Grafton, IL 62037

Also by Larry Wright:
HAPPY AS A CLAM
And 9,999 Other Similes
Published by Prentice Hall

THE GRAFTON GALLINIPPER
Magazine (1992-1994)
Published by Larry Wright

Second Edition

This is a genuine **Gallinipper Enterprises** publication

Acknowledgments

My sincere thanks to the sources listed in the bibliography. I am especially indebted to the good people listed below whose expertise helped make this book possible.

Scott R. Ballard
Illinois Department of Natural Resources,
Division of Natural Heritage, Alton, Illinois

K. L. Drews, Refuge Manager
Mark Twain National Wildlife Refuge,
Calhoun County, Illinois

James Herkert, Project Manager
Illinois Endangered Species Protection Board,
Springfield, Illinois

Scott Isringhausen
Park Interpreter, Pere Marquette State Park,
Grafton, Illinois

Charles and Pat Mayden
Piasa Photo, Alton, Illinois

John G. Mendoza
U.S. Dept. of Interior Fish & Wildlife Service,
Springfield, Illinois

Alice Lang-Runzi
Illustrator
Grafton, Illinois

Dutch Schoultz
HVS & Associates,
Clayton, Missouri
Typesetting, maps, layout and professional editing

Contents

Dedication

To Matthew, Katherine, Kelly, and Brooke

May you catch the warm thermal updrafts of life
and let them lift you
to your highest and noblist goals.

— Pop Pop

As each winter comes, we anxiously await the return of the American Bald Eagle to Grafton. When these beautiful birds extend their giant wings, the gentle winds blowing across the Mississippi and Illinois Rivers, lift them high into the heavens where they soar in effortless ease.

We are reminded of the scriptures in Isaiah 40:30, "They that wait upon the Lord shall renew their strength; they shall mount up with the wings of eagles".

As the Lord lifts up these majestic birds in flight, He can also lift us up and carry us through this life.

– Charles M. Schwaab
Grafton, Illinois

About the Author

Larry Wright was born and raised in St. Louis County, MO. In 1990, when Larry retired, he and his wife, Marg, built a new home 50 miles north of St. Louis in Grafton, Illinois. The home is situated high atop a bluff overlooking the confluence of the Mississippi and Illinois Rivers.

Since 1978 Larry has watched and studied American bald eagles and became enamored with them. From his excellent blufftop vantage point, he can actually look down upon eagles as they soar by his home and view them through binoculars or a spotting scope as they dive for fish and roost in the trees along the river.

In 1992 Larry became the first guide for Eagle Tours sponsored by the Alton Visitors Center.

In February, 1995, he was featured in a CNN special on eagle watching in the Grafton area.

From 1978 to 1993, he watched a steady growth in the wintering bald eagle population. But, since 1993 he has seen an enormous increase in the number of eagles in the area. Larry: "Back in the late 1970's we would usually count a dozen or so eagles on the Great River Road between Alton and Grafton (14 miles). Since 1993, on a good cold winter day, it was not uncommon to see over 100 eagles along that same route. This great increase in population has brought on a whole new tourism season for the entire River Bend area. People come here from just about everywhere to enjoy our eagles!"

Larry has written this book from a layman's viewpoint, not that of a scientist or professor. I find the book is a well organized handbook, easy to read, and is certain to introduce many to new and fascinating winter fun. He's got me hooked on bald eagles!

— *Dutch Schoultz*
Clayton, MO

Introduction

Nothing in my many years of enjoying nature compares with watching American Bald Eagles. The more I have studied them the more I'm captivated by these bold, strong, majestic, totally-in-charge birds. And the biggest thrill is to receive a close-up stare from those round, yellow, staring, piercing, don't-mess-with-me, eyes. We can be proud that the bald eagle is our national emblem.

We are so very fortunate to have the opportunity to seek and watch this king of birds right here in the heart of America. The more you study them as they roost, soar, fish, and play, the more you will want to return again and again.

This book is not intended to be a textbook. There will be no tests at the end of each chapter. It was published with one thought in mind — to help eagle watchers, whether first-timers or seasoned eagle-ogglers, to enjoy the fun and sport of eagle watching.

I have attempted to furnish true facts and you will note in a few areas that "eagle experts" don't always agree on some traits about this imposing bird. For basic statistics such as wingspan, mating habits, etc. I have relied on information from many sources and have attempted to give you what seems to be the *most* accurate. Reader, if you find any fact or statistic herein you feel is incorrect I would be happy to hear from you with substantiation for correction in the next edition.

There is a deep satisfaction in observing one of God's creatures in the wild. The bald eagle is one of His finest examples. As you begin your eagle watching trip I hope you will enjoy, as I have so many times, this awe-inspiring gift we can all share time and time again.

— *Larry Wright*

There are approximately 60 species of Eagles in the world but only two are found in North America — the Golden Eagle *Aquila chrysaetos* and the American Bald Eagle *Haliaeetus leucocephalus*. They are about the same size. The bald eagle is the only eagle living exclusively in North America. The only bird of prey larger than the eagle is the California Condor, an endangered vulture.

Since golden eagles are very seldom seen in this area, this book will be devoted almost entirely to bald eagles.

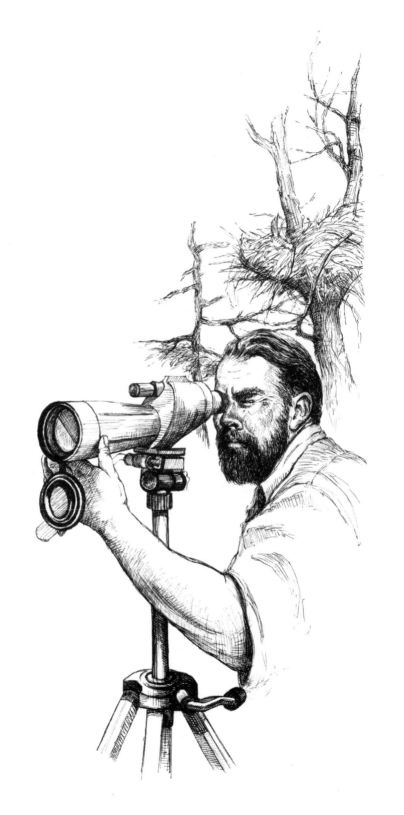

Chapter 1

SPOTTING EAGLES

Eagle watcher's paradise • Weather • Keep your distance • Early birds see the birds • Train your eye • I.D. Chart • Vultures • Binoculars & Spotting Scopes • Photographing eagles • Conducted tours

You're in the right spot!

You are now in one of the prime areas in America for spotting wintering bald eagles! The rough boundaries of this eagle watcher's paradise begins downriver from Alton at the mouth of the Missouri River, extends up the Mississippi to the Winfield Lock and Dam and up the Illinois River to Pere Marquette State Park.

So, check your calendar and make plans for a day of eagle fun between December 1 and March 1. Pack your gear (see Eagle Watcher's Pretrip Check List on page 10), dress properly for the temperature, check the Route Maps in Chapter 2 and head for eagle country!

Take friends along!

Eagle watching is more fun when you can share with others the sights and thrills that our national emblem will provide. Take your spouse, kids, friends, neighbors, senior citizens. Young and old alike will enjoy the outing because the entire tour can be appreciated from inside a warm car if you don't wish to walk on a winter day.

But first check with the weatherperson

The best time to look for eagles is during cold weather on a clear morning. On damp, foggy mornings eagles will be found perched in trees along the rivers, or, if a front has moved through and the weather is clear and windy, they will be soaring above the palisades. Frozen river conditions will find them standing on the ice on the river and backwater lakes of the region. More eagles will be spotted when the rivers freeze over than when not frozen.

Don't select a warm winter day to look for eagles!

Few eagles will be seen on warm winter days except early in the morning. On such days, by mid-morning, they will head for areas on the side of hills where the sun will not hit them and it is cooler. On warm, sunny winter days, they will often spend the entire day roosting in those trees, out of the eagle watcher's view.

Start early
Eagles leave their night roosts at sunrise and head straight for fishing waters (the Mississippi, Illinois, and Missouri Rivers and backwaters). By around 10 a.m. most eagles have stopped fishing and will be found perched in trees conserving their energy. The trees will be close to water. With their keen eyesight, they can see ripples in the water made by shad which swim near the surface. If they are hungry for a snack they will leave the perch, dive down, catch the fish with their razor-sharp talons, and often return to the same roosting spot.

Don't try to get too close
You will be doing the eagles a great favor if you will keep your distance between you and them. If you have good binoculars and/or a camera with a telephoto lens you won't need to get real close to enjoy the birds. Eagles are very sensitive to even minor disturbance.

If you park your car under a tree in which an eagle is roosting, stay in the car. Chances are, if you open the door, the eagle will fly away. This would be needlessly frightening the bird, making it waste precious energy flying off.

And, as a friendly reminder —

FAIR WARNING #1:
a person convicted of harassing an eagle faces up to a $20,000 fine and/or a year in prison. *So, please don't try to get too close.*

Binoculars, a must!
Binoculars are a must accessory for eagle watching. I am certainly no expert on optics, but I can recommend the following after some trial and error.

My binoculars are Minolta 10 x 50 power with a field of view of 410 ft. at 1000 yards. Cost was around $100. I have found this power to be maximum for hand held binoculars; most bird watchers prefer 7 x 35 power but for eagles, 10-power is better. I can hold the 10 x 50 steady by anchoring my thumbs against my cheek bones or, if in my car, rest my elbows on a window base.

Spotting Scopes, nice to have along

I received expert advice about scopes from Pat and Chuck Mayden at Piasa Photo in Alton. They recommended a Nikon IIA Spotting Scope with a quick variable zoom feature from 15 power to 45 power.

A good, solid tripod is important when purchasing a spotting scope. Mine is a Midas Tri Pod which collapses fairly compactly into a vinyl carrying case. Total cost for scope and tripod was around $490. But you can find excellent spotting scopes for a lot less — or a lot more!

Train your eagle eye!

After you have begun your tour and have spotted a few eagles, your eye will "know" what to look for. The chart on pages 6 and 7 will help your eye "find" eagles and determine whether they are adults or immatures. This chart is important in learning the shapes of large raptors of the area. Refer to chapter four for more descriptions and characteristics of bald eagles.

The Big Question
Is It An Eagle Or A Vulture?

Since vultures head south (from here) about the time eagles arrive from the north, it is rare to see vultures and eagles here at the same time. And their timing in the spring is the same. However, in the warm months, many people see vultures and mistake them for eagles.

BALD EAGLE IDENTIFICATION CHART

IMMATURE BALD EAGLE

The immatures will appear in a variety of plumages, determined by the age of the bird. The first year bird is nearly solid dark brown and is sometimes mistaken for an adult golden eagle (very rarely seen in this area). Second-year birds are lighter brown with spatterings of white on the underwings and tail. In the third and fourth years the birds start looking more like adults until, in the fourth or fifth year, they develop the full white head, neck, and tail feathers.

Unlike the adults, immatures' bills and eyes are brown. The feet are lemon-yellow. Size of immatures and other characteristics are similar to adults.

MATURE BALD EAGLE

White head, white tail, dark body, wings held horizontal (flat) during flight, body length, males up to 3 feet, females up to 3 1/2 feet, wingspan: Males: 6 to 7 feet, females up to 8 feet.

It's neck and tail are also white. The rest of the feathers are brownish-black in color. The eyes, bill, feet, and bare leg parts are bright yellow. The word bald comes from the Old English word "balde", which means "white" and refers to the white feathers covering the head of the mature bald eagle. Indeed, the adult American bald eagle is easy to recognize by its snowy white head that appears to be bald when viewed from a distance.

VULTURE & HAWK IDENTIFICATION CHART

TURKEY VULTURE

They vacation down south — not seen here during the winter months while eagles are present.

Dark body, light patches near wing tips, long black tail, gliding position held in V, small featherless red head, body length 2 1/2 feet, wingspan 5 1/2 to 6 feet. The vulture has a very short neck — the head appears to be attached directly to the shoulders (the eagle has a longer neck and larger head).

RED-TAILED HAWK

Rusty-red tail, cream to buff colored breast, abdomen streaked with brown, body length: 19 to 25 inches, wingspan: 4 to 5 feet.

Eagles — Males vs. Females

The females are larger and stronger than the males. The males are faster and more agile than the females. It is very difficult to tell the sexes apart since the bald eagle is "monomorphic" — the sexes look alike. The only time you can tell the difference is when mates are flying together and you compare their sizes. Other monomorphic birds: Gulls and most hawks.

Eagles in flight

In flight, the head and neck are stretched forward. They fly with deep strokes on flattened wings. The snowy-headed rulers are "beauty in flight" with their graceful movements, swiftness, and total control. They use the winds and currents to their advantage, soaring on thermals, diving with tail fanned, working the currents at low as well as high altitudes.

The key differences in Eagles Vs. Vultures

You can distinguish flying eagles from flying turkey vultures. Here are the points to look for:

Wings in flight: The eagle's are horizontal; vulture's are V-shaped.
Wing span: The eagle's slightly wider than vulture's.
Head: The eagle's is larger and covered with feathers; the vulture's is small, red, and bare.
Neck: Eagle's is longer.

When tourists, during the warmer months see turkey vultures and think they are seeing eagles, most Grafton locals, being of kind nature, agree with the visitors that the birds they are seeing are, indeed, eagles. After all, Grafton relies a great deal on tourism dollars.

Incidently, the turkey vulture was given its name by early Pilgrims because of the vulture's head is so similar to the head of a turkey.

Photographing eagles

To photograph eagles is, indeed, a difficult task, especially if you are trying to take a close-up or fill the frame with image. The main problem you will run into is trying to get close enough to the bird without scaring it away. In order to achieve this one needs a high power lens (i.e. 500 mm) or a spotting scope with a camera mount attachment.

These items will vary in price depending on the quality desired. Samyang makes a 100-500 mm zoom lens for manual focus cameras for about $329 that is excellent. Tamron, another lens maker, makes a 200-400 mm lens for auto focus cameras and A2X converters for about $659 and $184, respectively, that will give the photographer 800 mm zoom.

A spotting scope will be more powerful than 800, however they won't have as good a resolution. These scopes are used more for viewing than photographing. Either of these lens types can be put with manual focus or auto focus cameras depending on what the individual has.

If you are just beginning to do this type of photography you would be happier with auto focus over manual focus. Auto is so much easier to use and the results are excellent right from the first roll. Either camera type is very reasonable to purchase, starting at $199 for manual or $299 for auto focus.

Camcorders are an excellent way to record your day among eagles. I won't pass along any advice on using them — you probably know more than I do! Some people get some fantastic shots with plenty of action. I pan too fast!

CONDUCTED EAGLE TOURS
If you would like to be guided on an eagle tour before you take off on your own, there are several available. Here are three of the best.

"Eagle Tours" sponsored by the Greater Alton/Twin Rivers Convention and Visitors Bureau, Alton, IL
For information call: 1-800-258-6645 or (618) 465-6676.

"Eagle Watch" sponsored by The Nature Institute, Alton, IL.
For information call: (618) 463-0766

"Bald Eagle Watch" sponsored by Pere Marquette State Park.
For information call (618) 786-2204.

Chapter 2

ROUTE MAPS

The five maps in this chapter will lead you to some of the best eagle watching spots in the country!

———•••———

Before You Leave Home — Be Prepared!
EAGLE WATCHER'S PRE-TRIP CHECK LIST
1. Dress warmly according to the weather predictions.
2. Binoculars (a must).
3. Spotting scope and tripod (a good idea but not a must).
4. Camera (don't forget film!) and telephoto lens if you have one.
5. Tripod for camera (it will impress others).
6. Good boots, preferably water proof.
7. Bird field guide for identifying the many sea gulls, ducks, hawks, and other fowl you're certain to see.

MAKE SURE YOUR EAGLE TOUR IS A SAFE ONE

Safety Tip #1 to the _Driver_ and _All Passengers_
Before you start your tour, the driver and all passengers should buckle their seat belts.

Safety Tip #2 to the _Driver:_
For your safety's sake and that of others, do not read these maps while your car is in motion. Always take someone along to act as navigator and eagle spotter. **KEEP <u>YOUR</u> EYES ON THE ROAD**

Safety Tip #3 to the _navigator_:
If you see an eagle, you do not want the driver to slam on the brakes! It will infuriate the driver of the car behind you and, unless he/she has fast reflexes, you might end up with the front of a Buick in the trunk of your Hudson!

If you see something you want the driver to see, **very calmly** say to the driver: (A German or British accent might help.)

"Please engage your right turn indicator, then carefully and prudently pull over onto the shoulder. There is something I wish to point out to you <u>after</u> we have come to a complete stop, the gear shift is in Park, and your flashing caution lights are on."

Then point out the item of interest to the driver.

Another navigator's duty is to keep a count of the eagles spotted. At the end of the trip fill in figures and other data on the Field Notes pages begininng on page 68.

Each Route Map is followed by important information such as:
    √ Good eagle watch sites.
    √ Instructions on where to slow down, turn, stop, go, look, etc.
    √ Points of interest.
    √ Sights to see.

Where to start your eagle tour
Through my experience in taking many groups on eagle tours,
I highly recommend you <u>begin your tour at the Great River Road in Alton and drive the 14-mile scenic-friendly miles to Grafton.</u> This

affords you plenty of open water, air, and bluffs to train your eye for spotting eagles for other Routes. In a "good eagle year" a hundred eagles have been spotted on the 14-mile stretch, as many as 12 in one tree...but not on every trip!

But, you are on your own and can take the routes in any order you wish. Eagle watchers from St. Charles County might wish to start their tour by crossing the Winfield Ferry (if it is not closed due to ice).

Each of the five Route Maps are scenic and will provide plenty of eagles and other birds to enjoy. And it is not necessary to take all five Routes in one day. In fact, I don't recommend you do. Save Routes for another outing. You can come back to eagle country time after time!

Helpful hint
Before heading upriver on the Great River Road, stop at the Alton Visitors Center at Broadway and Piasa Street (see Route Map No. 5, page 30) where you can pick up a wide assortment of River Bend visitor information. You'll also find souvenirs. And restrooms (which may be the real reason most people stop in!).
Open daily 8:30 to 5:00. Phone: 1-800-258-6645 or (618) 465-6676.
Ask about their Guided Eagle Tours.

As you begin looking . . .
Some eagles will be roosting in the trees along the road or high up the bluffs. Others will be soaring just above the bluffs or perhaps a thousand feet higher than that. And keep an eye on the river where they dive for fish. And if you are really lucky, you'll be out when the river is frozen — that's when they are the easiest to spot. They will stand on the ice, sometimes alone and at other times in groups of 4 to 8 or more.

Eagle, *n . An adept fighter pilot,*
a fighter pilot who has shot down
many enemy planes

-Dictionary of American Slang

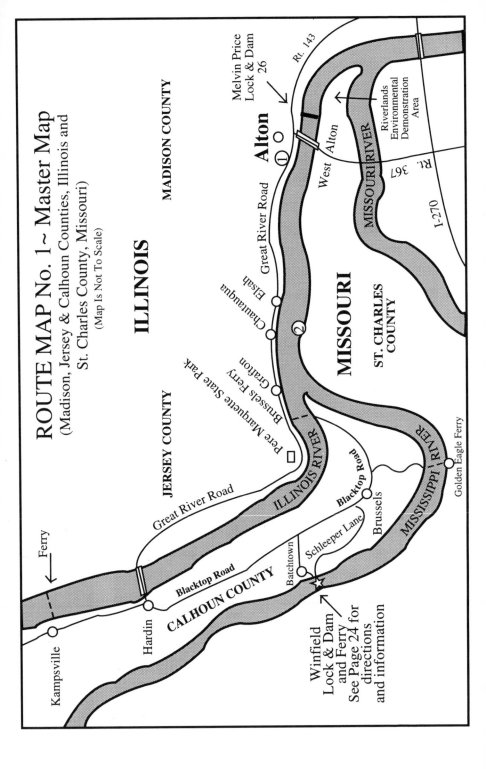

ROUTE MAP No. 1~ Master Map

(Madison, Jersey & Calhoun Counties, Illinois and
St. Charles County, Missouri)

(Map Is Not To Scale)

ILLINOIS

MADISON COUNTY

JERSEY COUNTY

CALHOUN COUNTY

MISSOURI

ST. CHARLES COUNTY

Kampsville

Ferry

Hardin

Blacktop Road

Great River Road

Pere Marquette State Park

Brussels Ferry
Grafton

Chautauqua

Elsah

Great River Road

Alton

Melvin Price
Lock & Dam

Rt. 143

26

West Alton

Riverlands
Environmental
Demonstration
Area

Rt. 367

I-270

MISSOURI RIVER

ILLINOIS RIVER

MISSISSIPPI RIVER

Blacktop Road

Brussels

Schleeper Lane

Batchtown

Golden Eagle Ferry

Winfield
Lock & Dam
and Ferry
See Page 24 for
directions
and information

14

ROUTE MAP NO. 1
Points Of Interest

If you set your odometer at zero at the stop sign at ConAgra, the odometer readings below will be very helpful.

• The Great River Road **(1)**, completed in 1965, with its majestic palisades, is one of the most scenic 14 miles of highway in America. Eagles can be seen soaring over the Mississippi and along the palisades as you travel upriver towards Elsah and Grafton.

• Vadalabene Bike Trail. A paved trail which runs along the Great River Road beginning in Alton and ending at Pere Marquette Park. A popular bike and hike trail and ideal for eagle watcher's to get some exercise as they enjoy the birds.

• The Blue Pool is **on your right about 2.2 miles upriver from Alton.** It is the first stone bluff you'll come to after the 55 MPH sign. Pull over on the right shoulder just past the guardrail. This is a popular day-roosting spot for an eagle or two and sometimes a red-tailed hawk. Check for them near the top of the bluff. Don't look for a blue pool, it was drained some time ago.

• Clifton Terrace Road is **4.4 miles** from Alton, at stop lights. There will soon be a public rest stop with restrooms at this site — perhaps by the autumn of 1996.

• Lockhaven Road is **6.5 miles** upriver from Alton. Pull over on the shoulder of the road **1/2 mile past** Lockhaven Road. Look back downstream and you might see several eagles in trees overhanging the river. This is also a spot where hundreds of seagulls often congregate and float on the river (or stand on it if frozen solid). On your return trip from Grafton you'll get a better view of this area.

• Slim Island **(2)**, across from Chautauqua, **12.3 miles** from Alton. This is the site of the nest built in 1992 described in Chapter 9. The nest is near the top of a tree that is near the far right end of the island as you view it from the Great River Road.

• The next town is Grafton, **14 miles** from Alton.

Other Great River Road area sights and activities:

• The Village of Elsah, 10.8 miles from Alton, is the first entire community to be listed in the National Register of Historic Places. Drive through Elsah. You probably won't see any eagles, but you'll see a truly quaint town with 19th century charm.

If you're hungry

For early risers, I recommend stopping for breakfast in Alton, Grafton or Pere Marquette Lodge. For lunch you'll find a large selection of restaurants and cafes in Alton, Elsah, Grafton, Pere Marquette Lodge, Brussels, Hardin, Kampsville, and Batchtown.

OVERNIGHT VISITORS

To get an early start, why not stay overnight in eagle country!

Bed and Breakfasts in the Area:

Tara Point Inn, Grafton (on high bluff, fantastic view!)
   (618)786-3555

The Corner Nest, Elsah (618) 374-1892

Green Tree Inn, Elsah (618) 374-2821

The Homeridge, Jerseyville (618) 498-3442

Jackson House, Alton (618) 462-1426

Maple Leaf Cottage, Elsah (618) 374-1684

Shafer Wharf Inn, Grafton (618) 374-2520

Wildflower Inn, Grafton (618) 786-3447

And the pride of Jersey County;

Pere Marquette Lodge, Grafton (618) 786-2331

Tara Point Inn Bed & Breakfast

Tara Point Inn is the home and bed and breakfast of Marg and her spouse, Larry Wright (author of this book). It was named after the ancient Irish mythical king's castle situated atop a high hill. With little advertising, the Inn, a hobby/business, has become a very popular place to relax and get away from the rat race or human race. Many guests tell us the Inn has the most spectacular view in the midwest. The view also provides great opportunities to watch bald eagles during the winter months and an excellent home base for eagle watchers.

Sorry, the driveway to Tara Point Inn is narrow and is for the use of **registered guests only.** Brochures are available at the Amoco Station and most shops and restaurants in Grafton.

For reservations or information call (618) 786-3555.

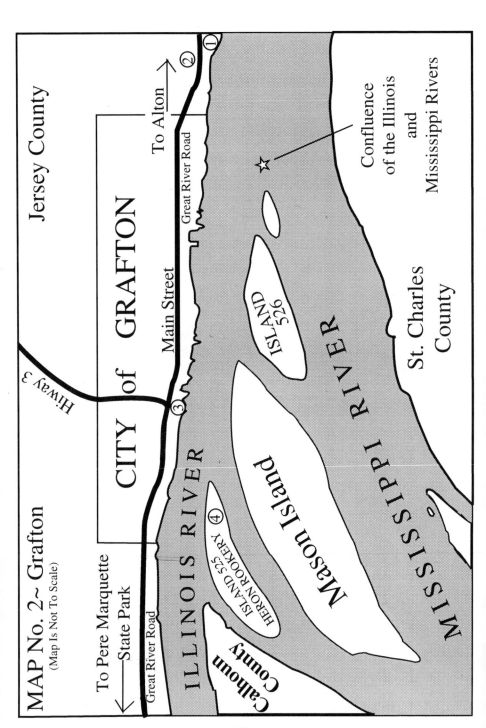

MAP No. 2~ Grafton
(Map Is Not To Scale)

Jersey County

CITY of GRAFTON

Hiway 3

To Alton →

Main Street

Great River Road

To Pere Marquette
State Park ←

Great River Road

ILLINOIS RIVER

Calhoun County

ISLAND 525
HERON ROOKERY ④

Mason Island

ISLAND 526

MISSISSIPPI RIVER

Confluence
of the Illinois
and
Mississippi Rivers

St. Charles
County

①
②
③

18

ROUTE MAP NO. 2
Points Of Interest

• After you pass the Raging Rivers Water Park, be alert for eagles in the trees along the river **on your left** when the road curves **to the right (1)**. Also, check out the old Grafton Quarry **(2) on your right** for a lone eagle near the top of the rock wall. This is the future site of a new Grafton rest stop with visitor information and restrooms. It is scheduled to be completed by January, 1997.

• Grafton Public Small Boat Launch **(3).** Turn left off Main Street at Highway 3. Drive to the river's edge for views of eagles roosting in trees on the islands across the river and perhaps some on the Grafton side. This spot also provides a beautiful view downriver of the palisades and upriver at the islands.

• A Blue heron rookery (heronry) is located on Island 525 **(4)** across from Grafton at the west end of Main Street (Highway 100). The hundreds of nests at the top of the trees stand out very clearly in winter months.

Other Grafton area sights and activities:

• Several delightful antique, craft, fudge, woodworking, and other specialty shops, restaurants, and hot fish stands.

• Chateau Ra Ha Winery.

• Grafton Amoco on Main Street (gas, groceries, pizza) open 24 hours, 7 days a week.

ROUTE MAP No. 3 ~ BRUSSELS FERRY & SOUTH CALHOUN COUNTY

(Map Is Not To Scale)

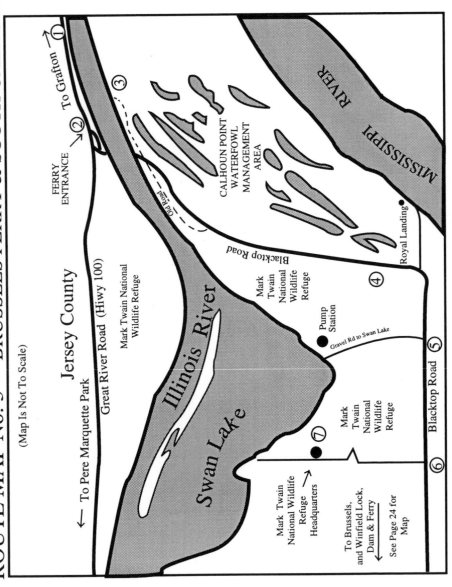

To Grafton →

① ② ③

FERRY ENTRANCE

Jersey County

← To Pere Marquette Park

Great River Road (Hiwy 100)

Mark Twain National Wildlife Refuge

Old Road

Blacktop Road

CALHOUN POINT WATERFOWL MANAGEMENT AREA

MISSISSIPPI RIVER

Royal Landing

④

Mark Twain National Wildlife Refuge

Pump Station

Gravel Rd to Swan Lake

⑤ Blacktop Road

Illinois River

Swan Lake

⑥ ⑦

Mark Twain National Wildlife Refuge

Mark Twain National Wildlife Refuge Headquarters

← To Brussels, and Winfield Lock, Dam & Ferry

See Page 24 for Map

ROUTE MAP NO. 3
POINTS OF INTEREST

After your visit to Grafton, stay on the Great River Road heading west (upriver). There will be little, if any, eagle activity for the next mile. Then the road curves left and you begin seeing the Illinois River and tall trees at its bank.

As the navigator checks these trees for perching eagles, the driver should give his/her full attention to the road because of several dangerous curves in this area.

• At **1.7 miles** from Grafton you will come to a green sign that reads, "Brussels Ferry 1/3 Mile", if the navigator sees eagles, drive into the **pull over area on the left** where you can park. **(1)**

If you don't see eagles, **keep driving** and around the next curve you will come to a second green sign, "Brussels Ferry 500 feet". If the navigator sees eagles the driver can **pull into a small parking area on the left or right side of the highway.**

At these pull over areas, stay in your vehicle. If you step out the vehicle door the eagle(s) will fly away.

The closer you come to the ferry, the more you are likely to spot eagles.

• You will then continue to the ferry entrance **(2).** As you pull in, **bear to the left.** Park your car in the closest lane to the river or follow "Eagle Parking" signs if they appear.

From here you are likely to see more "close-up eagle activity" than any other site in eagle country depending on weather conditions and the time of day — the earlier the better. Check out the trees just downriver to your left, several of which are dead. Also watch for eagles soaring and diving for fish. Park a while here and get out of your vehicle if you wish.

Dozens of seagulls (mostly herring and ring-billed), and sometimes an eagle or two will follow the ferry across the river and swoop down and grab small fish churned up by the ferry's large props. Watch eagles fish and also steal small fish from seagulls. As at other stops where you are fairly close to eagles, try to listen for their "chitter call".

• Now, cross the **Brussels Ferry** (free) into Calhoun County (a three-minute voyage). **Don't go straight ahead** on the Brussels blacktop highway, but instead, <u>immediately after debarking ferry</u>, **turn left on the gravel road.** You will often find eagles in the trees above the road or at the river's edge and also a great blue heron or so along the river's edge. Follow the gravel road for **.6 mi.** and you will arrive at the **waterfowl check station shack (3).** This is a good spot to get out and stretch your legs.

You will be within the Calhoun Point Wetland Recovery Demonstration Area. The area consists of a 2,200-acre tract of "aging" wetlands designated for restoration by the Corps of Engineers in conjunction with other agencies.

• After you have had enough fresh air, backtrack on the gravel road and **cross** the blacktop road at the ferry landing and **continue on** past the ferry landing on the gravel road. You might see eagles in the trees above the road, but most likely you will see several in trees across the river or flying above the river.

This one-mile road will curve to the left and bring you back to the Brussels blacktop highway.

• **Turn right** and travel **1.8 miles** (just before the road bends to the right) slow down and **turn right into a <u>small</u> parking area.** You will be within the Mark Twain Wildlife Refuge **(4).** Look over the fields on your right — you might see a flock of 1,000 to 5,000 snow geese. You also may spy an eagle or hawk in the taller trees.

The Mark Twain National Wildlife Refuge provides an undisturbed rest area for waterfowl, bald eagles and other birds. The refuge is closed to hunters year round.

• **Continue** on the blacktop road for **.8 miles** and **turn right (5)** on a gravel road and drive to its end. (If the road looks extremely soft and muddy you might want to omit this sidetrip from your tour.) I call this **Gravel Road to Swan Lake.**

NOTE: <u>This road is closed from October 15 until December 15</u>

as is the entire Mark Twain Refuge except for Refuge Headquarters.

Watch the field on your right for flocks of geese feeding on corn furnished by the conservation personnel. Also, check the trees on the left of the road for hawks and eagles. Further along you will see muskrat mounds on both sides of the road. At the end of the road at the Pump Station, if the ground is frozen (not muddy), park and walk the short path to Swan Lake. The lake is often frozen over and you will usually see eagles standing on the ice far out on the lake. Also, eagles will be perched in the trees along the lake's bank.

• Return again to the blacktop road and **turn right** and continue for **1 mile. Turn right at the first white house on your right (6)** which will place you on Hagen Road. Sign on the left side of the highway reads, "Mark Twain National Wildlife Refuge Headquarters".

Follow the "Refuge Headquarters" signs **one mile** to the Visitors Center **(7).** This center is a well kept secret to most people and is a highlight of my eagle trips. You will enjoy the viewing deck with its powerful scope and a wide expanse of prairie grass, trees, and Swan Lake in the distance. Several large trees, killed by the 1993 flood, have been left standing in the field as day roosts for eagles and hawks. You'll likely see ducks in the wetland field and snow geese in Swan Lake.

A variety of wildlife literature is available inside the building along with a nature display and video tapes including an excellent one on bald eagles. Restrooms are available. The center is open daily. For information, call (618) 883-2524.

NOTE: From this point you have two choices:
A. Return to the blacktop road and <u>turn left</u> and go onto Map No. 4. Take this route if you are running short of time.

B. Return to the blacktop road and <u>turn right</u> and go to the Winfield Lock and Dam. (Allow one hour for this round-trip.)

IF YOU DECIDE TO DRIVE TO THE WINFIELD LOCK & DAM, HERE ARE THE DIRECTIONS: (See Route Map No. 1, page 14)

Turn right and you will reach Brussels in 3 miles. Continue through Brussels and **stay on the blacktop road.** After passing through Brussels, **drive one mile** and you will see a green sign on the right, "Winfield Ferry" — **turn left here.** This road is called Schleeper Lane. Continue on this blacktop road for **5.4 miles** and you will see another green Winfield Ferry sign, **turn left** here and drive one mile.

YOU HAVE NOW REACHED THE WINFIELD FERRY AND THE WINFIELD LOCK AND DAM #25

There is always a lot of action to enjoy at the Winfield Lock and Dam! Its an excellent spot to watch eagles soar and fish for stunned shad below the dam.

You'll see plenty of eagles from the Illinois side, but for real action you need to take the ferry (for a fee) across to Missouri — from the ferry boat you will look back at the Illinois shore and sometimes see eight or ten eagles roosting in one tree. On the Missouri side, there is a viewing platform which provides an excellent vista of the lock and dam and eagles soaring and fishing.

Other Calhoun County sights and activities:
• Golden Eagle Ferry
• Kampsville Archaeology Museum. For information, Call (618) 653-4316.
• Kampsville Inn; great food!
• Whitman Hotel. This old inn, bar and restaurant was built in the mid-19th century.

Eagle day, n . *Payday. WWII Armed Forces slang use in reference to the eagle on U.S. banknotes and coins; also the eagle is popularly said to scream on payday.*

-Dictionary of American Slang

ROUTE MAP No. 4 ~ Gilbert Lake & Pere Marquette Park Area

(Map Is Not To Scale)

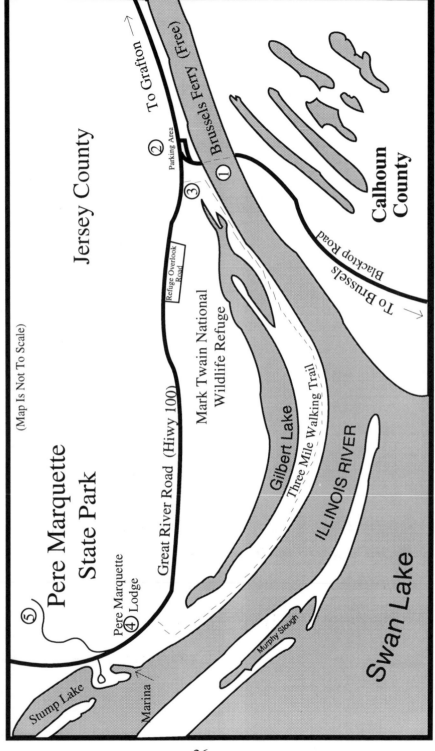

ROUTE MAP NO. 4
Points Of Interest

Drive back to the Brussels Ferry **(1)** and cross to the Jersey County side.

• The Gilbert Lake hike:
It is a good three-hour walk and you might wish to save it for your prime goal for a one day eagle watching trip.

But, if you decide to take the hike, park your vehicle across the highway from the ferry exit **(2)**. After you park your vehicle, then **carefully walk across the highway.**

I must emphasize that this is a dangerous section of the highway and I cannot stress enough the importance of being alert before crossing the highway. After crossing the road, walk upriver about 200 yards to a gravel road **(3)** which heads toward the river. Follow that gravel road and it will take you on the three-mile walk through the Gilbert Lake Refuge to Pere Marquette Lodge. (THIS AREA CLOSED FROM OCTOBER 15 - DECEMBER 15.)

If any of your group is not up to the hike, he/she could drive the vehicle to Pere Marquette Lodge **(4)** for a hot drink and wait as you make the walk.

Some of the most serious eagle watchers in the area rate this walk as the best way to see a lot of eagles. If you walk silently, you will see eagles perched in tall trees and on the ice of the river and lake, which is often the case by mid-January.

However. . .
If you don't want to take the three mile hike (six miles if round trip) **turn left as you exit the ferry** onto the Great River Road and drive **2.6 miles**. Pere Marquette Lodge will appear on your right. **Drive 100 yards past the park entrance** down the marina area **on your left.** An eagle or so can usually be found in the tall trees along the river. Also, look over Stump Lake to the **right of the marina**. You'll usually spy several varieties of ducks and other waterfowl here among the lily pads and duck blinds.

• Drive through the hills of the park **(5)**, keeping an eye out on the top of tall trees. There are several vista pullover areas. Park your car and enjoy a great view of the Illinois River and Calhoun County. And if you would like to take a short, yet very scenic hike, park your vehicle at Twin Shelters and walk the Red Trail (Hickory). This is a short 3/4 mile hike which includes two beautiful viewing points; McAdams Peak and Goat Cliff.

<u>Other Pere Marquette Park area sights and activities:</u>

• Pere Marquette State Park is the largest and the flagship of all Illinois parks. 8,000 wooded acres overlooking the Illinois River and Calhoun County. Several hiking trails provide varying degrees of challenge.

• Pere Marquette Lodge, built in the late 1930's by the CCC, is an excellent place to get warm and enjoy a meal. The Sunday brunch is great! For lodging or dining reservations, call (618) 786-2331. Off the lobby you will find a nice shop with quality gifts and souvenirs.

• For hiking trail information and hiking maps, stop at the log cabin Visitors Center.
Or Phone (618) 786-2204.

FROM HERE DRIVE DOWNRIVER
ON THE GREAT RIVER ROAD TO ALTON

Eagle eye, n . Figuratively one who sees or watches as well as an eagle, known traditionally for its keen vision

-Dictionary of American Slang

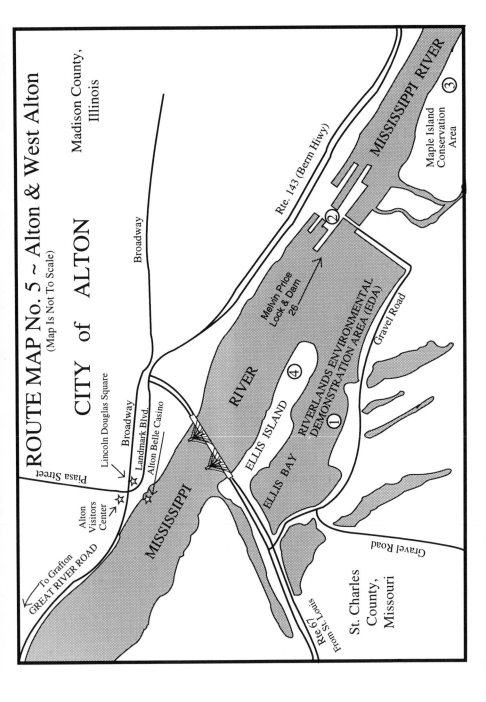

ROUTE MAP No. 5 ~ Alton & West Alton
(Map Is Not To Scale)

CITY of ALTON

Madison County, Illinois

Broadway

Lincoln Douglas Square

Broadway

Landmark Blvd.

Alton Belle Casino

Piasa Street

Alton Visitors Center

To Grafton
GREAT RIVER ROAD

MISSISSIPPI

RIVER

Melvin Price Lock & Dam 26

Rte. 143 (Berm Hiwy)

MISSISSIPPI RIVER ③

Maple Island Conservation Area

②

ELLIS ISLAND

④

ELLIS BAY

RIVERLANDS ENVIRONMENTAL DEMONSTRATION AREA (EDA)

①

Gravel Road

Gravel Road

Rte 67
From St. Louis

St. Charles County, Missouri

30

ROUTE MAP NO. 5

POINTS OF INTEREST

• "WETLANDS AREA" **(1)** known officially as the Riverlands Environmental Demonstration Area (EDA). **Enter EDA from Highway 67 on the Missouri side.** Coming from St. Louis it will be the last right turn you can make before crossing the new Clark Bridge (there is a service station here).

EDA consists of a 1,200 acre wetland site which the Corps of Engineers has restored to pre-settlement conditions. It features 800 acres of wet to wet-mesic native prairie and 300 acres of shallow marsh which create a natural type of riparian habitat rarely found in the Midwest.

EDA, a wildlife sanctuary, offers excellent opportunities for viewing a large variety of waterfowl, shorebirds, and marsh birds as well as other wildlife. Here you might catch a glimpse of the federally endangered peregrine falcons and kestrels (commonly called sparrow hawks).

108 eagles were counted in the EDA wetlands area in West Alton on a cold January day in 1994. If the ponds in the wetlands are frozen over you'll see several eagles standing on the ice.

• Follow the gravel road to the Lock and Dam. You'll find a parking area with views of the downriver side of the lock and dam where eagles soar and fish. Check out the trees on the Missouri bank of the river where there is usually a sizable group of day-roosting eagles. From this spot you also have a good view of Maple Island **(3)**, a very popular day-roosting site.

Melvin Price Lock & Dam #26 **(2)** is the largest construction project of the U.S. Army Corps of Engineers. You'll almost always find eagles on the downriver side of the dam.

Also drive the other gravel roads in the EDA area.

• Trumpeter swans. A group of 4-6 trumpeter swans have been wintering the EDA for the past few years. They can usually be found in the Ellis Island **(4)** area but they move around. They attract bird lov-

31

ers and photographers — so look for a group of ogling people and that's usually where you'll find the swans (or something else well worth ogling).

• Return to Highway 67 and **cross the Clark Bridge to Alton.** When you reach the Illinois side, **turn right** — you will be on Highway 143 (Berm Highway). Drive **2.2 miles to the stoplight** and **turn right.** The view of the lock and dam and Maple Island is very good from this vantage point. On most days, however, eagle watching is better from the Missouri side.

Other Alton area sights and activities:

• If you didn't stop at the Alton Visitors Center at the beginning of your tour, you should do so when you return downriver from Grafton. Return to page 12 for information.

• Lovejoy Monument, honoring Elijah P. Lovejoy, abolitionist editor who was killed 1837 by an angry mob while protecting his press. This is the state's tallest monument and is located at the Alton City Cemetery, 5th and Monument Streets.

• Lincoln Douglas Square and statues. Here, in 1858, the last of the famous debates took place. Located at Broadway at Market Street near the Alton Belle Casino.

• Alton Antique District, with dozens of shops, many on Broadway.

• Robert Wadlow Statue located on College Avenue. The statue is actual size of the tallest man in history (8 feet 11.5 inches) who died in 1940.

Mileage Chart

Alton to Clifton Terrace Road:	4.4 miles
Alton to Lockhaven Road:	6.5 miles
Alton to Elsah:	10.8 miles
Alton to Chautauqua:	12.3 miles
Alton to Grafton:	14 miles
Grafton to Brussels Ferry:	2 miles
Grafton to Pere Marquette Park:	5 miles
Grafton to Katmandu:	8,617 miles
Brussels Ferry to Brussels:	8 miles
Brussels Ferry to Winfield Ferry:	16 miles
Brussels Ferry to Pere Marquette Park:	2.8 miles
Pere Marquette Park to Alton:	21 miles

Eagle, n . (pl.) Insignia of a colonel in the U.S. Army

-The Random House American Dictionary

Chapter 3
WINTER MIGRATION
Why here? • ETA • Migration • Flight speed

Why they migrate south
Bald eagles migrate to our area primarily from widely separated breeding areas in Michigan, Wisconsin, Minnesota and Ontario. When the northern lakes and rivers freeze over and they can no longer find fish they head south for open waters and a winter vacation. They do not travel as a family group.

Why wintering eagles are so populous in this area
Eagles migrate and stay for the winter in the Mississippi/Illinois/ Missouri River area for three reasons:
1. Plenty of open water in which to fish.
2. Undisturbed roosting areas, both day and night.
3. Large geese and duck populations.

Of our lower 48 states, Illinois and Missouri have more wintering bald eagles than any other states. Nearly all bald eagles in Illinois are found near the Mississippi or Illinois rivers and make up the greatest eagle concentration in the continental United States.

Very few eagles migrate east of the Mississippi Valley.

When they fly south
Bald eagles begin arriving here in very small numbers as early as

October.

On October 27, 1995 at 7:31 AM I saw my first bald eagle of the season. It was mature and flew about 50 feet out from our front window at eye level (i.e., about 300 feet above Mississippi River level).

I was exhilarated! However, it is early December before good numbers are seen in this area. The peak time to see eagles here is from mid-December to mid-February. By early March most have left for the north.

An eagle lover in northern Minnesota has nesting eagles on his property. He notes that young eaglets, hatched in early May will begin migration south around October 1. That's only five months after hatching! They depart for the warmer clime <u>before</u> the parents! Somehow, even though they have never been more than a few miles from their nest, they find there way hundreds of miles south to spend the winter! Some experts feel the family will reunite as a group when they have all arrived at their winter home area — others are not certain.

Speed during migration

Eagles are capable of flying up to 300 miles in a day. However, fall migration is leisurely, perhaps 20 or so miles per day. Therefore, the flight from southern Ontario to Grafton, for example, would take about 35 days.

When the eagles move south, for the most part, they accompany the southward movement of waterfowl upon which they are prey. Since waterfowl stop at numerous "favorite rest stops" where they may pause for days to feed before continuing south, many eagles follow suit. So, from October through December, a leisurely, rest-then-continue flight southward occurs, eagles following flocks of geese.

Spring migration back north is much faster — they're in a hurry to get to the "happy breeding grounds."

Eagle, n . An American gold ten dollar piece, first coined in 1795

-Dictionary of American Slang

Chapter 4
<u>CHARACTERISTICS</u>

**Physical Stats • Speed/acrobatics • Sense Organs • Calls •
Lifespan • Great Flood of '93**

<u>Body length</u>

Males: up to 3 feet
Females: up to 3 1/2 feet

<u>Wingspan</u>

Males: 6 to 7 feet
Females: up to 8 feet

<u>Weight</u>

Males: 8 to 10 pounds
Females: 10 to 14 pounds

<u>Talons/Bills</u>

Eagles have very sharp, curved talons for grasping and killing the prey they eat. Their feet and talons are the size of a man's hands. Their yellow bills are curved, very strong and are used for tearing animals apart for dining after they are killed. (See Chapter 4, FOOD, for further information about how eagles use their talons to kill their prey.)

<u>Air time</u>

Eagle experts say that eagles will spend about 5% of the daylight hours in the air. To save energy, the balance of the day is spent roosting.

<u>Speed & Acrobatics</u>

Bald eagles have been clocked at 30-50 MPH in level flight and over 100 MPH in a dive. Eagles will perform rolls and loops in flight.

Often, pairs of eagles will tumble together in the air with talons hooked. This is called "taloning" which some say is "playing" and others say is "flirting". Still others feel these exciting free-fall descents are encounters between residents and trespassers. More on this interesting subject in **Chapter 9 Mating.**

Eyesight

Their eyesight is 5 or 6 times sharper than human's! While in flight, they can see a field mouse from a distance of 200 yards. Eagle writers and watchers have described their eyes in many terms, all of which I agree; *fierce, haughty, fixed and staring, icy stare, intensity of gaze, alert, bright*, etc. The simile, "Eyes like an eagle", is hundreds of years old.

Sense of Hearing

Compares with humans.

Sense of Taste and Smell

Poorly developed. Perhaps that's why they can stand to eat putrid food?

Calls

Bald eagles are generally silent. However, their "chitter-call" can sometimes be heard where groups of birds are active, like at our area locks and dams and ferry crossings. The sound can be described as a fast repetition of chirping sounds — like a call you would expect from a much smaller bird. Sometimes in flight you will hear a completely different sound, like a shriek or loud cry. I can't describe the sound in words, but you have heard it in nature films since you were a kid and when you hear it "live" you will recognize it. I did.

They also use a "nesting call" which I've never heard and would be rarely heard in Illinois or Missouri.

"Their voice is weak-metallic, squeal-like, gull-like, but broken in a series of notes. They also grunt." (Illinois Department of Natural Resources)

Life span

Depending on which eagle expert you listen to, bald eagles live to be 20 to 30 years in the wild and 30 to 50 years in captivity.

Flood effects on eagle day roosting

Before the Great Flood of 1993, I very seldom saw eagles in the trees along the banks of the Illinois on the Grafton side of the river. Too much human activity. But a dozen could be seen roosting on islands across the river where there are no homes.

Nearly 100 homes in Grafton were damaged beyond repair by that flood. These abandoned homes, in the FEMA Buyout Program, were not demolished until late fall of 1995.

Interestingly, during the winters of 1993-94 and 1994-95, though the abandoned homes still stood, eagles roosted in great numbers in the trees along the Grafton river bank. I assume the eagles sensed the absence of human activity in and around those deserted buildings. Perhaps they sensed that the buildings were empty of humans, and, therefore, they would not be disturbed by people-activity.

In the winter of 1995-1996, after the buildings were razed and the property became green space, eagles continued to roost along Grafton's bank of the river.

Eagle, n . In the game of Golf, a score of two under par on any but a par-three hole

-New Webster's Dictionary of the English Language

Chapter 5
<u>FOOD</u>

Daily dining delights • Airborne killers • Petty larceny • Survival of the fittest • Scavenging • A better place to fish by a dam site!

<u>Daily specials</u>

Eagles are diurnal raptors. Diurnal means they are active during the daytime. A raptor is a bird of prey, meaning the majority of their diet consists of meat. They are members of the group of fish-eating eagles known as "sea eagles".

Bald eagles feed primarily on fish and waterfowl, but may eat rabbits and other small mammals, especially during migration or in winter, when water is frozen over. Fish make up to 90% of their diet during nesting.

<u>Airborne killers</u>

Their principle means of offense are their large, dagger-clawed feet, with which they grasp and pierce prey such as fish. Small fish are sometimes eaten while the bird is in flight. Large fish will be carried to a tree to be eaten. When fish are abundant, other food sources will be ignored.

<u>Stop thief!</u>

They will often rob other birds, such as seagulls of the fish they catch. They also steal from other eagles - strangely, the food transfer usually takes place without a fight! Attempts to steal food from another eagle while in flight is called "pirating" and can result in some spectacular and fanciful aerial maneuvering.

Survival of the fittest
When fish are not available, eagles turn to waterfowl, preferably crippled ones. Crippled waterfowl (often injured by hunters) are of such important supplement to the fall and winter food that most observers feel that numbers of eagles fluctuate with the number of waterfowl in the area. Eagles are capable of carrying the equivalent of their own weight in flight. This is especially true when they ride thermals, the updrafts allowing them to carry a heavy load.

Bald eagles will harass a flock of ducks or geese into flight, then isolate a cripple or slow-reacting individual and the deadly game of predator vs. prey begins. Subsequently the prey is killed and eaten. Eagles prefer geese over duck. I do also.

A Grafton friend told me of watching, from a duck blind, an eagle killing a snow goose at about 500 feet in the sky. Death was instantaneous as the eagle's strong feet and sharp talons encircled and stabbed through the goose's neck. The dead goose was then dropped to the ground where it was consumed by five eagle-pals.

Flying with dead weight
In January of 1993, while guiding a group on an Alton Visitors Center Eagle Tour, we arrived at a large combined cornfield in Calhoun County where I often see thousands of snow geese and Canadas on the ground. On one particular day there were no geese in sight. We then spied three mature eagles in a white oak tree across the field. Then we saw an adult eagle flying laboriously, lugging a large snow goose with its talons.

Eagles weigh 8 to 14 pounds, snow geese weigh 8 to 10 pounds. The eagle flew about 100 feet at an altitude of around five feet, then landed and rested a few minutes. This process took place during a ten-minute period until the eagle had the goose over an embankment and out of our sight. It was then that the three eagles in the oak tree flew down to share a dinner of fresh goose.

Dive bombing
Local hunters in duck blinds have seen eagles swoop down at a duck

swimming atop the water. The duck will dive under water to escape attack. Often the eagle will dive and hover above the water until the duck is too exhausted to resist capture.

Scavengers

Eagles are expert scavengers. The bald eagle, except when food is scarce, rarely exerts itself by taking other than dead or disadvantaged prey...one of the reasons Ben Franklin favored the turkey as our national emblem. However, one must ask, are these eating habits due to laziness or cleverness? After all, it does take a lot more energy to chase down a flying goose or dive for fish than to take food that is available with no effort. Eagles will also frequent garbage dumps, if remote, and will eat of road kill such as putrid deer and other animals dead for several days.

"Wheresoever the carcase is,
there will the eagles be gathered together."
— New Testament

Eagles love locks and dams!

Bald eagles benefitted when the Army Corps of Engineers built 26 locks and dams on the Mississippi beginning in 1939. The water immediately downstream of the dams in our area is turbulent and keeps the water ice-free. The churning stuns fish, which rise to the surface to be picked up by low-flying eagles.

WANTED — Dead or Alive!

Some eagles fish directly from ice flows on the water. They will stand at the edge of the flow as it floats downriver (how else would it float?!), keeping an eye out for fish — dead or alive. Here again, this allows the eagle to conserve the energy required for flying and retaining body warmth during freezing nights.

Chapter 6
NIGHT ROOSTING
(Wintering Eagles)
Sleeping together • Do not disturb!

Night roosts are isolated

Communal night roosts are a unique characteristic of migrant bald eagles where they spend the winter. The birds crowd together in one tree, commonly accompanied by much dispute and juggling for position. James Lish, near the Salt Ford of the Arkansas River in Oklahoma observed 61 bald eagles using a particular night roost perched in one dead cottonwood.

Night roosts are usually in close proximity to the feeding area, but some will commute 10 to 15 miles. Freedom from human disturbances is an important factor in determining night roosting sites.

The specific perching sites at the night roost is almost invariably in a tree protruding above the general forest canopy, permitting both an unobstructed approach and takeoff. Freedom from small branches, often makes a dead tree the roosting site selected. The roosting trees are on the side of the hill that is best protected from the wind or in sheltered valleys and ravines.

Help protect night roosts

According to the Illinois Department of Natural Resources, the most important means of increasing bald eagle numbers is to protect areas used by wintering birds from human disturbance. Many people do not realize how sensitive bald eagles are to even minor disturbance. Although eagles may tolerate highway traffic passing regularly by a daytime perch, a human on foot is quite another matter.

FAIR WARNING #2

Birds at winter <u>night roosts</u> in particular may be in a very vulnerable condition and <u>should not be approached by anyone</u>. Being caught disturbing a night roost could result in a heavy fine and/or a jail term.

There are several night roosting areas in remote areas of Jersey and

Calhoun counties. Conservationists will not identify those locations.

As much as a half hour before sunrise, eagles begin streaming out of the night roost heading for feeding areas, not to return until dusk. However, the roost is seldom completely vacated. In fact, inclement weather may cause many of the eagles to remain perched there throughout the day.

Eagle, n . A reading desk or lecturn in the form of an eagle with expanded wings

-New Webster's Dictionary of the English Language

CHAPTER 7
DANGER OF EXTINCTION

Endangered • Threatened • Enemy No. 1 • Gunshot • Bounties • Pesticides • Lead Poisoning • History of protection legislation • YOU can help

"Endangered"

An *endangered* species is a plant or animal that is in danger of becoming extinct within all or a portion of its range. A species listed as *endangered* by the state of Illinois is in danger of disappearing as a breeding species in the wild within the state. If a species is classified as *endangered* by the federal government, the situation is even more grave. The species is in danger of becoming extinct within the entire country - possibly the entire world.

"Threatened"

When a species is listed as *threatened*, it is likely to become listed as *endangered*. This classification indicates that the populations are low enough and/or declining such that extinction is possible in the future.

Of the 500 species that are listed as *endangered* or *threatened* in Illinois, 28 are also listed by the federal government. The Illinois list breaks down as follows:

Plants: 356
Animals: 144 (29 fish, 9 reptiles, 3 amphibians, 43 birds,
              10 mammals, and 50 invertebrates (insects, mollusks).

Man is the eagle's worst enemy

Man, with his encroachment and disturbance of the eagle's natural habitat and other accidental or intended acts has become the eagle's prime enemy. Loss of habitat is the biggest long-term threat to bald eagle population throughout the United States. Human activities including agriculture, logging, and mining, have seriously depleted potential habitat. Land take over in the form of urban developments is eroding the eagle's "undisturbed space" and secluded areas for nesting. Only prudent management of bald eagle habitat, through partnerships with government, private organizations, and individual citizens will assure eagle protection.

Man's automobile has, over the years, taken its toll on eagles.

Others are caught in traps intended for coyotes and other animals. But several other human activities have been deadlier and more widespread.

Gunshot
Although eagles are now protected by law, gunshot by stupid, thoughtless people continues to be a principal cause of death. It is estimated by the Illinois Department of Natural Resources that shooting accounts for one-quarter of all reported dead eagles.

Over the years, from 1917 to 1962, untold thousands were killed with guns. It is estimated that more than a hundred thousand eagles were shot in the southwestern states. Between 1946 and 1962 at least twenty thousand golden eagles alone were killed by shooters.

Bounties
For many years, farmers and ranchers viewed the eagle as a threat to their livelihoods. In Alaska alone, over 100,000 dead eagles were turned in for cash between 1920 and 1940.

Why there were bounties on eagles
Earlier in this century, and much before that, it was thought that killing eagles was a good cause. After all, didn't eagles murder innocent lambs and calves? And didn't they carry off babies on occasion? (There is no recorded record in history of an eagle taking a human baby.) "The only good eagle was a dead eagle."

It took federal laws and continued public-relations and education to stop the slaughter
Changing the public's attitude towards eagles was a long and difficult task taken on by not only the state and federal governments, but also by naturalist writers, conservation clubs, and outdoor and conservation publications. The "killer" reputation and unfounded legends about eagles was slowly turned around. Unfortunately, the education came too late, after many thousands of goldens and balds had been greatly reduced in number and range.

And, even today, and perhaps for many years to come, there will be that handful of half-witted airheads who will shoot eagles, believing they attack livestock et al and are the "bad guys" of the bird world.

FAIR WARNING #3:
Bald eagles and their nests are protected by several federal laws, and

individuals convicted of killing eagles can pay fines of up to $20,000 and spend up to one year in prison. Concerned citizens who turn in eagle killers can receive government rewards of up to $2,500. In addition, violators face severe state penalties.

For centuries eagles were killed by native Americans for their feathers for headdress and claws as amulets, but it is unlikely that those traditions were responsible for a significant reduction in eagle population.

Eagles ARE the farmer's and rancher's friend!

Golden eagles and, to a lesser extent, balds, have always been a great benefit to farmers and ranchers. They prey on rabbits and other small herbivores, removing animals that compete with livestock for food. Most of the suspected livestock kills are not done by eagles, but are blamed on them because they are seen eating the carrion.

Farm pesticides took a terrible toll!

After World War II, man began using farm chemicals, especially chlorinate hydrocarbons, the most famous of which is DDT. These chemicals almost eradicated eagles entirely in the 1950's and 1960's. DDT was sprayed on croplands throughout the country and its residues washed into lakes and streams. There, they were absorbed by aquatic plants and small animals that were eaten by fish. The contaminated fish, in turn, were consumed by eagles. Those chemicals caused some eagles to be infertile. In others it resulted in producing thin eggshells which resulted in eggs being crushed in the nest during incubation.

By the early 1960s there were only 400 or so nesting bald eagle pairs in the lower 48 states.

As the dangers of DDT became known, in large part due to Rachel Carson's famous book *Silent Spring*, this chemical was banned for most uses in Canada in 1970 and in the U.S. in 1972. The banning of these pesticides, especially DDT was the turning point on bringing the eagle on the road to recovery, greatly increasing the number of eagles in the continental United States and Canada. Unfortunately, DDT is still used in Mexico.

Pesticides are STILL killing bald eagles!

In April, 1994 the Wisconsin Department of Natural Resources issued the following press release, which I have paraphrased:

PESTICIDE FOUND TO HAVE KILLED EAGLES IN BURNETT COUNTY
— Spooner, WI

A pesticide used to control insects in vegetables was responsible for the deaths of 17 eagles in northwest Wisconsin. The Department of Natural Resources and the U.S. Fish and Wildlife Service are offering a reward for information that leads to the arrest and conviction of anyone who caused the eagle deaths.

The pesticide, Carbofuran, was found in the eagles tested, authorities said. Carbofuran is considered an extremely potent pesticide that quickly kills once ingested.

A total of 17 eagles were found in Fish Lake in northeastern Burnett County. To assist the investigation processes the two agencies are offering a reward of up to $5,000 for information leading to the arrest or conviction of anyone who caused the eagle deaths.

To date (1996), nothing further has developed since the investigation began.

Power lines
It is unknown how many eagles are killed annually by collisions with power lines or electrocuted by high-power wires and transformers. Research has led to improved designs that reduce raptor electrocutions.

Lead Poisoning
Lead poisoning was identified as another widespread cause of mortalities in eagles.

In the 1950's, Wildlife Biologist, Frank Bellrose, conducted a comprehensive study showing the devastating effects of lead poisoning on waterfowl. Millions of ducks and geese died every year.

According to the U.S. Department of Interior, most cases of lead poisoning of eagles were the result of eagles feeding on hunter-killed or crippled waterfowl by lead shot.

Bald eagles do not get lead poisoning from lead in the tissues of lead-poisoned birds. They must actually swallow lead shot to get the disease. Although an eagle doesn't have a gizzard to grind down the lead shot, the strong acids of the stomach transform the shot into lead salts, which are

51

then absorbed into the blood and carried to various organs and tissues of the body. If enough lead is absorbed, the eagle gets lead poisoning and dies.

Thanks to Bellrose a campaign was initiated to outlaw the use of lead shot. But it was a slow process! Sadly, it was not until 1991 that lead shot was made illegal for migratory waterfowl hunting in all 50 states. Steel and bismuth shot are used in its place.

As with the outlawing of DDT, the ban on lead shot has been very instrumental in the eagle's comeback. Some states now have breeding bald eagles for the first time in many years.

Some eagle species in Europe have become extinct. Only the measures mentioned in this chapter have saved American eagles.

You can help save bald eagles!

• **Learn** more about the bald eagles.

• **Volunteer.** Write to the U.S. Fish and Wildlife Service or your State fish and game agency to learn more about volunteer work involving saving bald eagles:

U.S. Fish & Wildlife Service	Illinois Endangered Species
452 Arlington Square	Prot. Board
Washington, DC 20240	Lincoln Tower Plaza
	524 S. Second
	Springfield, IL 62701-1787

• **Join** a conservation organization that helps protect and enhance bald eagle habitat.

• **Report** any potential problems that might result in injury or death to an eagle or destruction of eagle habitat.

FAIR WARNING #4:

Federal permits are required in order to have in one's possession bald eagle feathers or parts. So, if you spot a feather on the ground and you think it might be from an eagle, let it lie. Don't pick it up! Being caught with one in your possession could mean a very stiff fine and/or a prison term!

LAWS AND EVENTS AFFECTING BALD EAGLES:

1782 The Continental Congress adopted the bald eagle as the central figure for the Great Seal of the United States.

1940 — Bald Eagle Protection Act prohibits, except under certain conditions, the taking, possession, and commerce in bald and golden eagles; penalties are one year imprisonment and/or a $5,000 fine.

1960 — National Audubon Society's Continental Bald Eagle Project; the first organized large scale attempt to census breeding eagles.

1963 - USDA Forest Service established the first management program for protection of bald eagle nesting areas.

1967 — The Endangered Species Act listed the bald eagle as *endangered* in the contiguous United States south of the 40th parallel.

1972 — Migratory Bird Treaty Act strengthened to further protect bald eagles.

1972 — Insecticide DDT banned from use in the United States with stiff penalties.

1973 — Endangered Species Act amended; defines taking of eagles as harass, harm, pursue, hunt, shoot, wound, kill, trap, capture or collect and prohibits taking; requires that no action authorized, funded or carried out by a federal agency shall jeopardize *threatened* or *endangered* species unless provided by special exemption.

1978 — Endangered Species Act, amended; bald eagle declared *threatened* in Minnesota, Wisconsin, Michigan, Washington, and Oregon and remained *endangered* in the rest of the contiguous states.

1981 — The Lacey Act makes it unlawful for any person to "import, export, transport, sell, receive, acquire or purchase" any bald eagle. Criminal penalties include fines up to $20,000 and/or five years in prison (a felony).

1984 — Northern States Bald Eagle Recovery Plan completed.

1995 — In August of 1995, Congress, acting on a USF & WS request, upgraded bald eagles from *endangered* to *threatened* in all lower 48 states except Arizona, New Mexico, and West Texas where its status remains *endangered*. Legal protection of bald eagles and their habitat will not change. Animals that are *threatened* are given the same amount of protection as those that are *endangered*. The terms *endangered* and *threatened* represent the threat of extinction, not the level of protection given to animals under the Endangered Species Act or other Federal laws.

Chapter 8
POPULATION

EAGLE COUNT OF BREEDING PAIRS OF BALD EAGLES

(Source: Illinois Endangered Species Protection Board.)

	(1) Illinois Breeding Pairs	(2) Illinois Eaglets Produced	(3) U.S. Breeding Pairs	(4) Illinois Winter Population
1963	0	0	417	
1973	1	0		
1974	2	0	791	
1975	0	0		
1976	0	0		
1977	0	0		
1978	2	2		
1979	2	0		
1980	3	1		
1981	2	2	1188	
1982	5	2		
1983	4	2		
1984	2	1	1757	
1985	2	1		
1986	3	2	1875	
1987	4	2	1657	936
1988	8	8	2475	1151
1989	10	4	2680	1442
1990	8	7	3020	1511
1991	9	12	3391	1988
1992	11	16	3747	2025
1993	12	12	4016	2124
1994	10	15	4449	2918
1995				2819

(1) = **Illinois Breeding Pairs** - the number of eagle pairs that initiated nests in the state.

(2) = **Illinois Young Produced** - the number of eaglets produced in Illinois.

(3) = **U.S. Breeding Pairs** - the number of breeding eagle pairs in the 48 contiguous United States.

(4) = **Illinois Winter Population** - estimate of the number of eagles that wintered in Illinois. Counts only include the Illinois side of the Mississippi River along the entire length of Illinois and the Illinois River from Peoria to the Grafton (the confluence with the Mississippi).

Note: Numbers in above chart represent <u>pairs</u> of adult bald eagles that are occupying a territory (nesting area). As juvenile bald eagles (less than 4 years of age) are not counted, the total number of bald eagles far exceeds these numbers.

Wildlife experts believe there may have been 25,000 to as many as 75,000 nesting bald eagles in the lower 48 states when the bird was adopted as our national symbol in 1782.

They're coming back in great numbers!

Today, the bald eagle has presence in every state except Hawaii, either as a nesting territory, permanent residence or a wintering area. In recent years, we have seen the population of bald eagles rebound greatly from the low levels of the decades prior to 1980. Alaska has the largest state bald eagle population with over 40,000 birds.

State and federal wildlife experts say the eagle is making a strong comeback since we began keeping poisons like DDT and lead shot out of the (eco) system and preserving habitats.

We are seeing more immature eagles each year which is a very positive sign of a growing population.

1963 is considered by many as a population low for bald eagles.

The chore of counting eagles

Over the years, various groups have conducted census-taking of bald eagles in Illinois and other states. In the 1990's in Illinois the Illinois Natural History Survey (INHS) seems to be the key census clearing house. INHA, with several state, federal agencies and private groups do their annual ground count during the same approximate days each January. Groups of counters are assigned to geographical sections so the same eagles are not counted two or three times.

Their counting system seems to be accepted by eagle scholars. But, to come up with a 100% accurate census would be almost impossible and the figures INHS provides give us a gauge to see the general increases in eagle population.

Quoting <u>Distribution and Abundance of Winter Populations of Bald Eagles in Illinois</u> by Stephen P. Havera and Glen W. Kruse:

"The difficulty of coordinating a census over a large area has resulted in counts that provide only an index to actual population levels.

"Nationwide bald eagle censuses have shown a dramatic increase since the late 1970s. The increase is attributed partially to more effective counts. Until 1976, counts were the result of incidental eagle sightings during the USFWS January waterfowl inventory. In 1979, the National Wildlife Federation (NWF) organized an annual midwinter bald eagle survey. Thousands of persons were involved in the enumeration of bald eagles.

"Variation in geographical coverage of the midwinter bald eagle surveys among years makes accurate counts difficult. . ."

Brent Manning, Conservation Director said, "It [the census] isn't intended to be an exact count of every eagle in the state, but gives us a number to compare to previous years' counts so we can judge how eagle populations are doing."

Sue Lauzon, Executive Director of the Endangered Species Protection Board, said counters try to complete their efforts within a two-day period to avoid counting eagles that move from one area to another.

"We conduct aerial surveys along the entire length of the Mississippi River and most of the Illinois River. We fly over islands and other areas that counters on the ground aren't able to get to. Also, we compare figures on areas that can be counted both from the air and on land, which helps give us a more accurate picture of population trends."

Nowhere are bald eagles more numerous than the Chilkat Valley of Alaska where more than 3,000 bald eagles congregate each fall to feed on the spent bodies of spawning chum salmon.

Chapter 9
MATING

The mating game • No divorces??

For many years it had been thought that only adults, when their heads and tails become white, will mate. However, several eagle watchers have reported seeing eagles without the full mature white head and tail mate with mature mates and successfully raise young. Ah, young love!

Very few breed in our area. Their breeding is done when they return in late February or early March to their homes in our northern states or Canada.

Some experts tell us that one stage of mating takes place in the air. An eagle finds a partner, soars to a high altitude and tries to dive piggyback with its mate. Sometimes they play tag. Some scientists say these acts (often referred to as "taloning") include actual copulation. Others say it is part of flirtation and merely precedes the actual act of mating. Just one more mystery about eagles that the experts don't seem to agree on.

But, generally, mating is done in or near the nest. When the female is ready for copulation, she makes a head-down bowing gesture, and the male hops on her back, with his talons closed so that she won't be hurt. As he flaps his wings for balance, her tail goes up, his down; contact takes place. The act is over quickly.

Mates for life? Who really knows?
Some scientists believe that a mated pair of bald eagles stay together until one dies. Other experts feel that mate relationships are relatively long-lasting but have no documented proof that they stay together for life. Still other observers feel that most eagles *seem* to mate for life. One study shows that some pairs stay together year-round while others might stay together except for the winter migration months.

Chapter 10
NESTING

Up in the eyrie • Nesting in Illinois • Slim Island nest
The great nest builders • Eggs • Cane & Abel syndrome

Returning north to nest

The eagles that migrate to this area each winter build their nests in Canada as well as northern U.S. states such as Minnesota, Wisconsin and Michigan. Some experts say a mating pair of bald eagles will return to the same *nest* every spring.

One says they return to the same *nesting area* year after year and will often maintain two or more nesting sites in the same area and rotate between the available sites. There are a few experts who say the mated adults *usually* return to the same *breeding territory* each year. Confusing. Its one more subject that is not universally agreed upon.

First Nests

An eagle's nest is called an eyrie. Bald eagles like to build their eyries in the top of sturdy, tall trees near the water. Sometimes they will nest on ledges of high cliffs. It is believed by some that, when they become adults, they will build their first nest within 100 miles of where they were raised. Others say the first nest will be in the same general area as where they themselves were hatched. Again, the experts have various of opinions.

Nest in peace

They have been known to share their forest with lumberjacks and to breed at sites if a 200-yard buffer is left undisturbed. Full time human residents and vacationers often occupy eagle habitat, such as shorelines, without disturbing the eagles as long as human population is limited and habitat such as nest trees, roosts, and feeding grounds are mostly undisturbed.

Nesting increasing in Illinois

For the first time in many years, the 1980s and 1990s saw bald eagles nesting in Illinois again even if in small numbers. Each year more nests are sighted. According to Margie Bjorklund, naturalist of the

61

Wildlife Prairie Park, there are now 16 to 20 nests statewide (1995) — up from none in the 1960s and 1970s.

A nest near Grafton on Slim Island

In March of 1992, a pair of bald eagles built a nest in a high tree on Slim Island which is a Missouri island 1.5 miles downriver from Grafton across from Chautauqua. Three eaglets, one male and two females, were hatched there in the spring of 1992 and left the nest healthy.

But, before they "flew the coop" . . .

In May of '92 The World Bird Sanctuary of St. Louis hired Robert Branson, a tree trimmer, to retrieve the eaglets for banding. When Branson arrived at the nest, "the babies waddled over to check me out. They ruffled their feathers and squawked to try to scare me away." He gently put the three birds into a bag and lowered them on a rope to the ground. Aluminum bands were placed on the eagles' legs and the babies were lifted back up by Branson and replaced into the nest. He described the nest as being, "as big as a grand piano, 6 feet across and 5 feet high. The eaglets were about 7 weeks old and each weighed about 7 pounds. The carcasses of 20 fish littered the nest and the odor was overwhelming."

Unfortunately, neither the parents nor babies returned to use the nest in the spring of 1993. Missouri Conservation agents placed warning buoys around the island warning boaters not to get near the island. Even so, human activity during the summer of 1992 in the form of boating near the nest site is blamed for the nest's abandonment.

Though the nest site was deserted, someday in the future, we may, through the I.D. bands, discover where the three eagles migrated or selected their nesting area.

In January, 1996 I noted with interest that the Slim Island nest appeared to still be in good condition and was being used as a "meeting place" for bald eagles. Often I spotted anywhere from two to five eagles in, on, and around the nest. In layman's terms, it seemed to be a "pad for the gang to hang out, rap and party."

Nest size

The nest at Slim Island was about average for a first year nest, though the "grand piano" simile may have been overstated. But eagle nests do become quite large. The pair starts the first year with a nest of sticks, weeds, grass, moss, bark and dirt. The first year nest is about 5 or six feet across and about as deep. Some sticks are often 5 feet long and almost as thick as a man's wrist. Some nests have been documented for over thirty years.

The Minnesota Department of Natural Resources located a nest 9 feet in diameter and 6 feet deep and it was only two years old. Another bald eagle nest in Alaska measured 8 feet across and 12 feet deep. Another was 10 feet across and 20 feet deep. The granddaddy and largest (and most written about) nest ever found weighed 4,000 pounds. The tree fell during a storm and the nest was placed on a truck and taken to a weight station.

Eggs

The female lays one to three (usually two) dull white eggs in March. Only one brood is raised each year. Both parents set on the eggs for an incubation period of 34 to 36 days. They both guard the nest, and bring food to the young. The eaglets are <u>ready to fly</u> in about 70 to 75 days after hatching.

The nestling stage lasts 10 to 12 weeks and the fledgling stage 3 to 4 months

Fratricide

The eggs usually do not hatch on the same day. This means that the first hatched has a head start on development. With a growth-rate of up to a pound about every four days, this gives the first-hatched a strength advantage over the second and third to hatch.

Spats between the chicks often occur in the nest, sometimes turning ugly. Nest observers have seen two eaglets fight over food scraps as the larger chick overpowers the smaller one and pecks and even starves the smaller sibling to death. While this conflict is taking place the adults stand passively by and watch the fratricide, seemingly unconcerned.

It is interesting to note that eaglets about to fledge are sometimes heavier than their parents. This is because of their aggressive feeding in the nest. All they do is eat and sleep, and, with no exercise, they become couch potatoes!

Chapter 11
BONUS BIRDS IN THE AREA

Other birds

During your safari in search of eagles, you can be assured of spying other birds that put the icing on any eagle watching cake. Look for the following birds common to our eagle country in the winter: (List furnished by the Brussels District Mark Twain National Wildlife Refuge.)

American Black Duck
American Crow
American Goldfinch
American Tree Sparrow
Barred Owl
Black-capped Chickadee
Bufflehead
Canada Goose
Canvasback
Carolina Wren
Common Goldeneye
Common Grackle
Common Merganser
Dark-eyed Junco
Downy Woodpecker
Eastern Screech-Owl
Great Blue Heron
Great Horned Owl
Hairy Woodpecker
Herring Gull
Horned Lark
House Sparrow
Killdeer
Lesser Scaup
Mallard

Mourning Dove
Northern Bobwhite
Northern Cardinal
Northern Flicker
Northern Mockingbird
Northern Pintail
Pileated Woodpecker
Red-bellied Woodpecker
Redheaded Woodpecker
Red-tailed Hawk
Red-winged Blackbird
Redhead
Ring-billed Gull
Ring-necked Duck
Rock Dove
Ruddy Duck
Snow Goose
Song Sparrow
Swamp Sparrow
Tufted Titmouse
White-breasted Nuthatch
White-crowned Sparrow
White-throated Sparrow
Wood Duck

A rare treat, if you are lucky, will be seeing **trumpeter swans** at the Riverlands Environmental Demonstration Area. See Route Map No. 5 on page 30

Chapter 12
OTHER EAGLES
Goldens • Eagles around the world

Only the bald and the golden eagles are found in North America. The golden eagle is also found in areas of northern Europe. The bald is found only in North America.

Golden Eagles

Very few goldens are spotted here each year. The golden eagle lives mostly in remote mountainous regions of our western states such as the Rocky Mountains. They dine mostly on rabbits and other small mammals, but also enjoy fish. You can tell a golden by its feet, which are feathered right down to the toes. Bald eagles, like other sea eagles, have bare legs.

Goldens are a bit stronger and more aggressive than balds.

Other types of eagles are found on every continent. There are over 50 species of eagles around the world, in such areas as Europe, Asia, Philippine Islands, East Indies, Australia and Africa. The Harpy eagle of South America weighs up to 20 pounds. The Monkey-eating eagle of the Philippines, as its name indicates, is powerful enough to carry off monkeys. The Little eagle of New Guinea is smaller than a Sea Gull.

Chapter 13
EAGLES AS SYMBOLS

The eagle has been a regal symbol since the third millennium before Christ. The Romans in 104 B.C. began using a golden figure of an eagle as their chief emblem which, to the Romans, stood for strength, skill, and bravery. Later, kings and emperors from many countries chose the eagle as one of their key figures of dominance. Centuries ago, the eagle was the bird of war in many European countries. A double-headed eagle was the imperial Russian and Austrian coats of arms. Even Hitler used the eagle on many Nazi official emblems. For a time during WWII his headquarters were in the medieval castle of Ziegenberg called Eagle's Eyrie.

Several countries, including Mexico include an eagle as part of their national flag design.

American Indians used the eagle as an important symbol for centuries before white man arrived. An eagle often tops totem poles in the Pacific Northwest.

The United States, by the Continental Congress, selected the bald eagle as our national emblem in 1782. In part, the document read, "Whereas by that Act of Congress and by tradition and custom during the life of the nation, the bald eagle is no longer a mere bird of biological interest, but a symbol of the American ideals of freedom . . ."

The bald eagle — what a perfect emblem of independence! But, at one point, Benjamin Franklin suggested the turkey instead of the bald eagle. Can you picture the family sitting down at Thanksgiving and dining on our national emblem?! Gratefully, he was well outnumbered by those who preferred the bald eagle.

The bald eagle is still the official U.S. emblem, a sign of independence, power, courage and freedom. Its picture is on the Great Seal of the United States (woven into the carpet of the Oval Office and never walked on, even by the President), the President's flag, and has been used on U.S. coins and paper currency.

Check a dollar bill, the Great Seal is on the back side, symbolizing sovereignty of the United States. The design consists of a bald eagle with outspread wings, a shield on its breast. The eagle holds an olive branch of 13 leaves and 13 olives in its right talon, and 13 arrows in its left. It prefers to live in peace, but can wage war.

Several states, including Illinois, include the bald eagle as the central symbol of their state seal.

Many private companies include the eagle in their corporate logos; Anheuser-Busch, for example. Uses of the eagle as a symbol include the U.S. President's flag, U.S. coinage, flagstaffs, medals, uniform buttons, currency, flags, banners . . . the list goes on and on.

The Great Seal of
Illinois

The United States
Presidential Seal

The Great Seal of the
United States

State Birds

The most popular state birds are:

Cardinal	7 states
Mockingbird:	5 states
Western meadowlark:	5 states
Bluebird:	4 states

While these are common in their particular states, other states honor lesser known birds, such as the scissor-tailed flycatcher (Oklahoma), lark bunting (Colorado) and the hermit thrush (Vermont).

It is surprising that not one of our fifty states honors the bald eagle (nor the golden eagle for that matter) as their state bird, considering the bald eagle is our nation's prime symbol.

———● ● ●———

I truly admire and 'look up' to our national emblem, the Bald Eagle. May this beautiful bird flourish and become 'native' to all fifty states, Canada, and Mexico.

Long after I am gone, perhaps this dream will come true for my grandchildren to enjoy, but, hopefully, never to be taken for granted.

— Larry Wright

———● ● ●———

FIELD NOTES

My Eagle Count Record

Date	Area Visited	Weather	Notes	Eagles Counted	
				Adults	Imm.

Date	Area Visited	Weather	Notes	Eagles Counted	
				Adults	Imm.

Date	Area Visited	Weather	Notes	Eagles Counted Adults	Imm.

BIBLIOGRAPHY, SOURCES OF ADDITIONAL INFORMATION & FURTHER READING

Bent, A.C., *Life Histories of North American Birds of Prey, Part 1.*, Dover Publications

Bird, D.M., *Biology and Management of Bald Eagle and Osprey* , Harpell Press, Canada

Dictionary of American Slang, Wentworth and Flexner, Thos. Y. Crowell Co., New York

Fishing & Hunting Journal, St, Louis, MO

Frederici, Peter, *Illinois Bald Eagles*, The Nature of Illinois, Fall 1992

Gieck, C. M., Life Tracks, Wis. Dept. Nat. Resources, Bur. of Endangered Resources

Illinois Department of Natural Resources

Illinois Natural History Survey, Biological Notes 129, February, 1988

Lincer, Clark, and LeFranc, *Working Bibliography of the Bald Eagle,* Nat. Wildlife Fed.

Mews News, World Bird Sanctuary, St. Louis, MO

New Webster's Dictionary of the English Language.

Savage, Candace, *Eagles of North America*, Northwood Press,Inc.

Sindelar, C.R., *Bald Eagles Amongst the Apostle Islands . . . ,* Wis. Dept. Nat. Resources

Stalmaster, M.V., *The Bald Eagle,* Universal Books

Stokes, Don & Lillian, *A Guide To Bird Behavior Volume III,* Little, Brown & Co.

The Random House American Dictionary

The Telegraph, Alton, Illinois

The World Book Encyclopedia

U.S. Army Corps of Engineers

U.S. Department of Agriculture, Animal and Plant Health Inspection Service

U.S. Department of Interior, U.S. Fish and Wildlife Service

U.S. Environmental Protection Agency

INDEX